LITTLE GOLDEN
Picture
Dictionary

BY NANCY FIELDING HULICK

PICTURES BY
TIBOR GERGELY

GOLDEN PRESS
NEW YORK

gb

Tibor Gergely's lively and amusing pictures have delighted children for many years. The very youngest children will love looking at this LITTLE GOLDEN PICTURE DICTIONARY—and the child who is learning to read will enjoy identifying each boldly printed word with its accompanying picture.

Twenty-Third Printing, 1971

airplane

The airplane flies high in the sky.

apron

The cook wears a yellow apron.

alligator

The alligator has sharp teeth.

ark

The ark floats on the waves.

alphabet

This is my alphabet book.

armchair

The armchair is soft and deep.

apple

The apple is red and ripe.

automobile

We went for a ride in the automobile.

baby

I have a baby brother.

bird

The early bird catches the worm.

barn

The cow is in the barn.

boat

The boat is in the harbor.

bear

Bears love to eat honey.

bread

I like to eat bread and butter.

bicycle

Can you ride a bicycle?

bus

We ride to school on the bus.

cake

There are six candles on the birthday cake.

chick

The mother hen has four baby chicks.

castle

The castle stands on the hill.

clown

We saw a clown at the circus.

cat

The cat plays with a ball of yarn.

coat

My coat is thick and warm.

chair

This is a rocking chair.

cow

The cow grazes in the field.

desk

I write at my desk.

donkey

The donkey says "Hee-haw."

doctor

The doctor cured my cold.

door

The door is open.

dog

The dog chews on a bone.

dress

I have a pink party dress.

doll

I like to play with my doll.

duck

The ducks swim in the pond.

eagle

The eagle is a proud bird.

elephant

The elephant likes to eat peanuts.

ear

I listen with my ear.

elf

The elf wears a suit of green.

eel

The eel swims in the stream.

engine

The engine goes *chuff chuff*.

egg

I had an egg for breakfast.

envelope

Daddy mails his letter in an envelope.

fairy

The fairy has a magic wand.

fish

The pet fish swim in the tank.

family

The family
goes for a walk.

flag

The United States has a new flag.

farm

We grow corn and wheat on the farm.

fox

The fox has a bushy tail.

fireman

The fireman wears a red hat.

fruit

There are many kinds of fruit.

garden

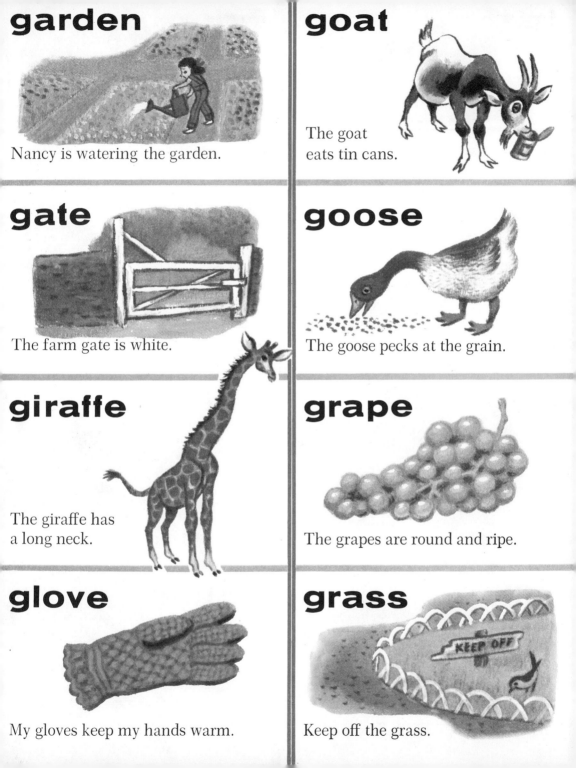

Nancy is watering the garden.

goat

The goat
eats tin cans.

gate

The farm gate is white.

goose

The goose pecks at the grain.

giraffe

The giraffe has
a long neck.

grape

The grapes are round and ripe.

glove

My gloves keep my hands warm.

grass

KEEP OFF

Keep off the grass.

hat

This hat is big and shady.

hoop

I like to roll my hoop.

helicopter

The helicopter can fly up and down.

horn

Little Boy Blue,
come blow
your horn.

hen

The hen sits on her eggs.

horse

The horse ran away.

hill

The hill is covered with flowers.

house

I live in a big house.

ice

Ice freezes in the icebox.

ink

We write with a pen and ink.

ice cream

I like strawberry ice cream.

insect

There are many kinds of insects.

igloo

The igloo is made of ice and snow.

iron

Mother presses my clothes with an iron.

Indian

The Indian wears a war bonnet.

island

The island is surrounded by water.

jacket

Bob's jacket
has long sleeves.

jam

Jam is good to eat.

jack-o'-lantern

The jack-o'-lantern is in the window.

jay

The jay flew away.

jacks

We like to play jacks.

jeep

The jeep can go fast.

jaguar

The jaguar has black spots.

juggler

The juggler juggles balls and hoops.

kangaroo

The kangaroo leaps high in the air.

kitchen

Mother cooks in the kitchen.

kettle

The water is boiling in the kettle.

kite

The kite flies high in the sky.

key

The key fits the lock.

kitten

The kitten laps her milk.

king

The king sits on the throne.

knife

The knife is very sharp.

ladder

The ladder is
for climbing.

lemon

Will you take lemon in your tea?

lamb

The lamb is white and wooly.

lettuce

Lettuce is
good in salads.

lamp

The lamp has a
nice red shade.

lion

I saw a lion
at the zoo.

leaves

The leaves are falling from the trees.

log

The cabin is made of logs.

mailman

The mailman has a letter for you.

monkey

The monkey swings from tree to tree.

map

The map shows countries of the world.

moon

The moon is full and bright.

milk

Milk is good for you.

mouse

The mouse likes cheese.

money

I keep my money in a purse.

music

I can read music.

name

My name is
DAVey

net

Billy caught the fish in a net.

nail

John hit the nail on the head.

newspaper

Daddy reads the newspaper.

needle

I cannot thread the needle.

nose

My nose is
for smelling.

nest

There are two eggs in the nest.

nut

A walnut is a nut.

oak

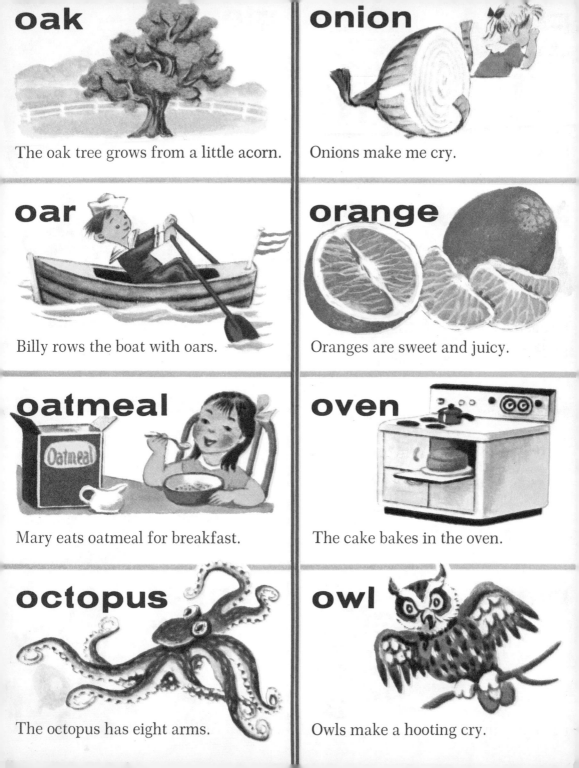

The oak tree grows from a little acorn.

onion

Onions make me cry.

oar

Billy rows the boat with oars.

orange

Oranges are sweet and juicy.

oatmeal

Mary eats oatmeal for breakfast.

oven

The cake bakes in the oven.

octopus

The octopus has eight arms.

owl

Owls make a hooting cry.

paint

Sally has a new paint set.

pie

Who took a piece of pie?

park

I walk my dog in the park.

pig

The pig has a curly tail.

parrot

"Hello," says Polly Parrot.

policeman

The policeman stops the cars.

piano

I can play the piano.

puppet

What a funny puppet!

quail

The quail lives
in the woods.

rain

The rain falls
in big drops.

quart

There are two pints in a quart.

ring

I have a pretty ring.

queen

The Queen is tall
and beautiful.

river

The boat sails on the river.

quill

The porcupine has sharp quills.

rooster

The rooster crows at dawn.

Santa Claus

Santa Claus carries a big pack.

skyscraper

There are many skyscrapers in New York City.

scarecrow

The scarecrow is made of straw.

sled

The sled speeds over the snow.

school

I go to school to learn.

snowman

The snowman has a carrot nose.

seesaw

The seesaw goes up and down.

squirrel

The squirrel likes to eat nuts.

table

The table is set for dinner.

train

The train is streamlined.

tepee

This Indian lives in a tepee.

tree

The tree has leafy branches.

tiger

The tiger has black stripes.

truck

DAIRY

The milkman drives a truck.

toy

I have a toy teddy.

turtle

The turtle has a hard shell.

umbrella

I carry an
umbrella in the rain.

Valentine

Be Mine

A friend sent
me a Valentine.

unicorn

The unicorn has one horn.

vase

There are
flowers in the vase.

uniform

The soldier wears a uniform.

vegetable

Corn and carrots are vegetables.

United States

We live in
the United States.

violin

The violin has four strings.

wagon

Bobby pulls his brother in the wagon.

wood

Daddy chops wood with an ax.

watermelon

I like to eat watermelon.

Xmas

Xmas is a short way to write Christmas.

web

This is a spider's web.

x-ray

The doctor x-rayed my chest.

window

There is a butterfly at the window.

xylophone

I have a toy xylophone.

yacht

A yacht is a big sailboat.

zebra
The zebra has black and white stripes.

yak
I saw a yak at the zoo.

zeppelin
David wants to ride in a zeppelin.

yard
The children play in the yard.

zero
The thermometer reads zero.

year
A year has 365 days.

zoo
Wild animals live at the zoo.